The Fortunes of John de Courcy

Direction artistique : Jamie Keenan
Mise en page : MCP

Enregistrements, montage et mixage : Studio Corby
Texte lu par Hester Wilcox

Dépôt Légal : 6858/01
Achevé d'imprimer par EMD S.A.S. en Juin 2010
N° d'impression : 23250

The Fortunes of John de Courcy

Philippa Boston

didier

AN HISTORICAL NOTE

Before the reign of King Henry VIII, in the 16th century, England was a Catholic nation. This, and the course of European history, changed when King Henry fell in love with a young woman named Anne Boleyn.

Denied permission to divorce his queen and marry Anne by Pope Clement VIII, the English king rebelled against Rome. In 1534, he founded a new, Protestant church with himself as its Supreme Head: the Church of England, or Anglican Church.

For the rest of Henry's reign, Catholicism was violently suppressed: monasteries were destroyed, churches stripped of their riches, and countless people who resisted the new religion put to death. In Oxford, the nation's pre-eminent university town, there were religious riots and strong resistance from inside the different colleges.

Under Henry's daughter, Queen Elizabeth I, it became a capital offence to resist Protestantism. Large numbers of Catholic students in Oxford were imprisoned, and many of the teachers fled to France. Ultimately, from the year 1581 (and for the next three centuries), all students at Oxford's colleges were required to subscribe to the 39 Articles of the Anglican Church.

This story takes place the following year.

Chapter 1

I

On the morning of December 20th, in the year 1582, the sun rose bright and clear over the university town of Oxford. Its light entered a window high in the walls of Christ Church College, and shone on the face of John de Courcy, who had fallen asleep at his desk the night before.

Woken by the light, he rose from the desk, massaging his neck as he crossed the room to open the heavy window. He looked out on the field where sheep and cattle stood on the ice-white grass. Across the field he could see the dark form of Oriel College, smaller and older than the other colleges of Oxford.

There were groups of students coming across the white field toward Christ Church College, where an announcement would soon be made in the great hall: the nomination of the Duke of Gloucester's new Scholar, a prestigious position that came with a good revenue. A position that many expected to go to him, John de Courcy.

"Hey, Johnny!" he heard the call of his friend, Harry Hopetoun, in the street below.

Harry was looking up at him, shading his eyes against the sunlight.

"What is it, villain?" John answered.

"Shut your mouth, vermin!" his friend smiled, "Are you ready for your hour of glory?"

"Harry, how can you tempt the gods by saying these things before the ceremony?"

"Because there is no greater philosopher in all of Oxford, my dear friend! Not even the vile, rat-faced Sir Edgar Hardridge can rival you. Before the day is finished you will be the Duke of Gloucester's Scholar and a rich man!"

"*Shhhh*. Harry, do be quiet."

But Harry had already entered the college,

running up the stairs to open the door of John's room.

"You must be more prudent, Harry," John reprimanded him. "There are ears everywhere in this college, and some would prefer that a Protestant such as myself did not become Scholar to the Duke. It is not long since blood flowed upon the streets of our town. Please, say no more until the nomination is over."

"Consider me silenced," Harry answered. "But you are wrong about this place. Christ Church College is Queen Elizabeth's fief: you have nothing to fear from the Catholics *here*! It is I, with my Catholic family, who must be careful, living as I do among the radical Protestants of Brasenose College!"

Harry examined John's appearance for the first time, saying "You look like you have slept in your clothes."

"I have."

"You must change!"

"My other clothes are being washed–"

"John de Courcy, I despair. This is the most important day of your life and you do not even have clean clothes? How do you expect to charm the lovely Miss Jane Mansfield if you smell like a horse? You will have to borrow something of mine. Come, we must hurry."

As they exited the room, they crossed the mute servant-boy, Tom. He waved crossed fingers at John and smiled nervously.

"Thank you, Tom!" John called as he ran down the stairs.

II

At that same moment, in another part of Christ Church College, four men were gathered in a secluded room inside the chapel. Three of them listened nervously as their leader spoke.

"We must be certain of our plan," he said. "You all understand your roles in this?"

The speaker's hat camouflaged a vicious, suppurating infection on the side of his face. He had none of the vanities of the age: wearing no colourful clothes, but only the ecclesiastical black robes of a Prelate.

The three men nodded.

"The Duke still has his suspicions about my

loyalties. He is not convinced that I have truly embraced the bastard Queen's... *Church of England*," the Prelate continued disdainfully. "My spies tell me that the Duke detects 'a lack of fervour' in me, and suspects that I remain true to our Holy Mother, the Church in Rome. That is why it is vital that he does not elect the godless John de Courcy as his Scholar. We need one of our people advising the Duke, such as Sir Edgar Hardridge."

"Can we be sure of Edgar Hardridge? He *is* the Duke's nephew, my lord," one of his men asked.

"Aye, but Sir Edgar has no love for Queen Elizabeth's blasphemous religion," the Prelate said. "The Queen is old and childless. In a few months she will be fifty. And when she finally joins the devil in Hell, the Duke of Gloucester will be one of the most powerful men in England. Guided by us, the Duke will install a Catholic king and we will have no more of this Protestant perversion."

The Prelate pulled the soft fabric of his hat further over his suppurating cheek as he spoke of perversion.

III

Once John was dressed in his friend's clean clothes, they left Harry's rooms at Brasenose College and walked down the High Street, its mud still frozen hard from the cold.

As they turned the corner onto Wheatsheaf Alley, they smelled the delicious scent of apples, cinnamon and cloves: the wassail vendor was there, fragrant vapours rising from his vat of hot liquor. Harry and John joined the crowd of students waiting to buy some of his infusion.

Harry touched John, drawing his attention to a figure standing before the door of a tavern not far away: Sir Edgar Hardridge was talking to someone hidden in the doorway. A soft arm appeared from the shadows, a woman's hand caressing Sir Edgar's cheek.

"A girl of infinitely bad taste," Harry whispered. John laughed silently.

The hand came away from Edgar's angular cheek, and John caught sight of a bright butterfly tattooed on the wrist. The colours of the butterfly stood out in the greyness of the narrow alley.

"It seems Sir Edgar is in love with a sailor," whispered John, taking the mug of wassail from the man and handing it to his friend.

IV

So many students were assembled in Christ Church that the great hall was warm despite the cold December morning. There were five days until Christmas, and the walls of the hall were decorated with branches from a holly tree: green leaves and scarlet berries giving a festive air to the room.

As the students remarked John de Courcy's entrance, they let him and Harry pass through them, acknowledging him as the favourite to win the nomination. Many shouted messages of good fortune and others slapped John's back as he passed, wishing him luck.

As John and Harry reached the front of the hall, the noise stopped. Sir Edgar Hardridge and his friends had entered the hall. Again the crowd parted to let them through, but no one touched the shoulder of Sir Edgar, and no messages of luck were shouted, although they all knew that if anyone was to beat John de Courcy to the prize, it would be Edgar, nephew to the Duke.

The door at the side of the hall opened and a herald blew his trumpet.

"Men of Oxford, welcome my Lord the Duke of Gloucester!" the Steward shouted as the Duke appeared, resplendent in a cloak of green velvet and a hat ornamented with ostrich feathers. The Duke smiled generously at the crowd as they cheered and applauded. Behind him came a procession of University dignitaries led by William Mansfield, the Dean of Christ Church College. Dean Mansfield's increasingly beautiful daughter, Jane Mansfield, took a seat on one side with her younger sister, Maude.

In spite of his anxiety, John could not take his eyes from Jane. She had never looked more fabulous. Her long, auburn hair cascaded down over the deep, red brocade of her dress. She caught his eye and smiled warmly at him. He could not breathe and the room was suddenly too hot, but he forced himself to look away from Jane toward the great Duke.

"A fine day for a fine occasion!" started the

Duke. "I have considered many talented young men, yet only one can be my Scholar. The Gloucester Scholar will receive 30 gold sovereigns, and a revenue provided by myself for as long as he continues his studies here at Oxford."

The crowd gasped, although they knew the value of the prize already. Little else had been discussed for many weeks.

"I am a soldier, not an orator, and so I will simply tell what you have all come to hear. It will come as little surprise. I have chosen John de Courcy as my Scholar for his brilliant..."

The rest of the Duke's words were lost in the noise that erupted from the assembled crowd. The ancient stones of the hall resounded with cheers and whistles and cries, hats flew high in to the air and strangers embraced each other.

Slowly, as though he were rising from the bottom of a lake, the noise penetrated John's confused thoughts. He turned questioningly toward Harry, whose face could barely contain the smile that split across it. Behind Harry's shoulder he saw the thunderous expression on the face of Sir Edgar. Only then did John realise what he had heard the Duke say: he had won the nomination. The Duke was smiling, holding his hand towards him. John felt a push at his back from Harry and he moved forward, took the proffered hand and stepped up on to the podium.

"It couldn't happen to a better man, John. You are as clever as they say that you are good and honest. I look forward to the great works you will no doubt produce." The Duke smiled and then turned to the crowd, holding up his arms. The crowd became silent.

"There is wassail for every man who wishes to drink the health of John de Courcy, Gloucester Scholar!"

The crowd cheered once more as servants arrived to fill the cups that stood on tables around the hall. John's eyes sought out those of Jane, whose face shone with happiness at his success. The Duke followed John's gaze and laughingly clapped him on the shoulder.

"She is indeed a glorious object of study, is she not? A very fine young woman, John. Maybe you will win more than *one* prize today!"

Chapter 2

I

THE EARLY MORNING SUN had stayed with the people of Oxford on that happy day, but its rays made no impact on the ice-white grass of the pastures between Christ Church College and the River Thames. After luncheon, Jane agreed to walk in the pastures with John, accompanied – at a distance – by his friend, Harry, her sister Maude, a page and the Mansfield sisters' maid.

All but the maid were happy with this arrangement.

Jane Mansfield was happy to be with the strange John de Courcy, so tall and yet so gentle, so handsome and yet apparently unaware of his charms. Her younger sister, Maude, adored Harry Hopetoun more than anyone in the world. Their fathers had been friends as children and the tradition had continued with Maude and Harry. No one could argue with her as well as Harry, no one made her laugh as Harry did.

John smiled happily at Jane, offering her his arm, which was gladly taken. Harry and Maude, no longer children, kept a strict distance between themselves as they talked. The maid followed behind, complaining to the page about the cold.

"I wish it was always so cold, Jane," John said, gazing at her, as they walked.

"Do you not like summer, John?"

"I do. But in summer you are not attired in red velvet that compliments the auburn glow of your hair..."

Jane laughed modestly, "Are you a poet as well as philosopher, John? "

"Only in your–"

They both looked up as they heard a sound of shouting and galloping horses. A group of riders were fast approaching along the river bank, the metal of the horses' shoes sparking on the hard ground.

"A race, sirs!" cried the page. "The gentlemen are racing!"

"Mercy!" said Maude. "This is madness! How can they make the horses gallop on this ice?"

The two front horses turned sharply up the avenue towards the college. As they did so the page jumped out with excitement, shouting and waving his arms about.

"Ice, sirs! There is ice!"

The third horse, disturbed by the sudden jumping of the boy, lost its balance on the frozen earth and ejected its rider, who fell hard to the ground. The figure of Philip Howard, Duke of Gloucester lay still, face down upon the earth. John and Harry rushed to him, carefully turning him over. John put an arm under his head and lifted him gently as Jane and her sister reached the scene. Jane took the Duke's bare hand in hers and rubbed it, but yelped as she scratched her hand on his large, emerald ring.

The Duke opened his eyes and squinted at them for a few moments.

"Was that noise from you, my lady?"

"Sir! You are alive!"

"I am indeed. How come I to be lying on the ground? Where is my horse?"

The maid handed Jane the Duke's glove and his cloak, both of which had come off in the fall. The Duke looked at them and then around himself.

"Your horse did not make the corner, sir. You fell. We were worried."

"I thank you for your worry, my lady. John de Courcy, you are already meriting your patronage, I see! Thank you, and young Hopetoun."

"Sir, it is nothing more than any would have done. We..."

"Uncle! What happened? Are you hurt? What did that idiot de Courcy do to scare your horse?" Edgar Hardridge had returned with the rest of the riders.

Jane frowned at him. "It was nothing to do with him, Edgar."

"You have the audacity to call *us* ridiculous, when you treat a horse like that on icy ground, Hardridge?" Harry sneered at Edgar.

"Now, now, gentlemen." The Duke held up a

hand. "This is not the place for your rivalries. These kind people helped me, Edgar. I am alive, but I confess that I am not completely well. If one of you men could help me to my feet..." John and Harry jumped forward to help the Duke, who walked a few tentative steps to establish he was not so badly injured as he thought, retied his cloak and replaced the glove.

"Remember, Harry Hopetoun," he said, getting on his horse, "that it was not just my nephew who was riding on the ice, but myself also. Would you say the same words to me?"

The Duke lifted an eyebrow at Harry whose face blushed red as he mumbled his apologies.

"No – you are right." the Duke smiled, "You spoke the truth as the man of law you are. It was foolish of us, and ended in disgrace for me. But I will survive! Until tonight's banquet then!" The Duke touched the horse's flanks and set off at a gentle speed up the avenue.

Edgar held out his hand to Jane.

"Would you do me the honour of accepting a ride back to the college on my horse, Miss Mansfield? You must be shocked and tired."

"No, sir, I thank you." Jane shook her head at Edgar very pleasantly. "Our walk was interrupted by the accident and I would like to finish it."

As John hurried to Jane's side once more, Edgar turned away. He looked briefly at the page, smiling, then whipped his horse hard and galloped after his uncle.

II

Some hours later, as the final preparations for the evening's banquet were completed, there was a great commotion in the Duke's chambers. His thunderous voice could be heard shouting furiously, and servants were sent running to his aid.

After his fall from the horse, the Duke had retired to his bed in the company of two young 'ladies' Edgar had procured to distract him from his injuries. Alluring and well-practised in the arts of love, the two whores had succeeded in their mission: distracting the Duke for the entire afternoon, with only a brief respite when Tom, the mute servant, brought a platter of refreshments to the door.

It was when the Duke dressed himself for the

banquet that the trouble started: he discovered that his Ducal ring, a jewel that had been in the Howard family for centuries, was not on the table where he had placed his pendant, bracelets and rings when the whores arrived. His instant suspicion was that one of them had stolen it, but after searching them intimately he was certain this was not the case. Nor could the servant, Tom, have taken it: he had not entered the room, but had passed the platter to one of the naked whores at the door.

This was when the servants were called and ordered to search the room from top to bottom, even looking for rat holes in case a rodent had taken the ring as the Duke cavorted with Edgar's whores. There was nothing.

"Are you sure that you had the ring when you undressed, sir?" Edgar asked when he heard the furore. "Perhaps you lost it earlier in the day. When you fell from your horse, for instance?"

Suddenly, the Duke was not certain. Had he or had he not placed the ring on the table? It was true that his glove had come off when he fell from the horse – could the ring have come off at that moment too?

III

The vast banquet hall of Christ Church College was lit by a thousand candles, in the chandeliers, on mantelpieces, on tables, in every niche, and among the branches of green holly with red berries that decorated the walls for Christmas. Priceless tapestries inlaid with golden threads were glowing in their light. The few ladies were dressed in their most beautiful dresses, the men magnificent in velvet doublets, brocade breeches and fur-lined capes.

The air was alive with laughter and shouts: spirits were high, in all except the Duke. The Gloucester Ducal ring had been given to the first Duke by the King himself, and was the most prized of all the family treasures. Philip Howard had seen the ring shine on the hand of his father. To him it was the emblem of manhood, of all that he had wanted to be.

Almost the last to arrive was John de Courcy, who entered the hall out of breath, red-faced and with his hair in disorder. He was followed by the figure of Edgar and some of his friends, all smiling widely.

“You are late, sirs!” the Duke barked “What kept you? I am not in the mood to be kept waiting this evening.”

“Apologies, my lord,” said John. “Sir Edgar and some fellows of his thought it might be amusing to drop me in the fountain. I resisted, fortunately, or else I would have been a great deal later than I am.”

“This is not the time of year to give a man a ducking, Edgar.” the Duke snapped, “What were you thinking of?”

“It was only a game, uncle. We did not intend to drop him in the water, only to make it seem so!”

“If that was a game, I’m a rat’s arse,” hissed John angrily, trying to tidy himself. He took the seat of honour in between the Duke and Jane, who thankfully did not look as bad-tempered as his new patron did.

IV

The tables were piled high with chicken legs and pies, bread and oysters, which the guests ate hungrily as the Rhenish wine was poured, and then platters of roast meats that were first shown to the Duke for his approval before being placed on the table: succulent roast beef, legs of lamb and venison joined the feast. For dessert, there were tarts and gingerbread covered in gold leaf.

The Duke was in no humour for talking until he had eaten. Only then did he turn his attention to John, who had been deep in conversation with Jane Mansfield, magnificent in a bodice embroidered with yellow thread.

"So John de Courcy, what plans do you have for your studies now?" he asked, "Or is my new Scholar's brilliant intellect to be monopolised by young ladies who tempt the Queen's anger by dressing in yellow?"

Jane, hearing the Duke's words, suppressed a smile. She knew that her dress was audacious, but how could a young woman obey Queen Elizabeth's rules on ladies' clothing? The queen had only made the rules so that nobody should be as resplendent as herself. But if the ageing queen was not there to see, and a young girl's beau was...?

"Maybe the lovely Jane should pay more attention to my nephew, Sir Edgar." the Duke smiled,

"As the wife of a noble you would be free to wear gold and silver threads, Miss Mansfield."

"It is true, sir, that only a noble's wife is free to dress so. But surely you do not think I pay attention to any man other than my father?"

"Ha! Do you hear that, Edgar?" the Duke laughed, "Mistress Jane knows how to play the game!"

John saw Jane blush deeply and felt the rush of blood to his own head as he resisted the desire to reprimand the Duke for his familiarity.

"Speaking of games, uncle," Edgar answered, "is it not time for some amusements? What say you to a little sport?"

The Duke, who was always in favour of such things, especially after a few cups of wine, slapped the table with his hand, silencing the hall. "An excellent suggestion! My spirits are returning! What game would you have us play, nephew?"

"Let me think, my lord..." Sir Edgar replied, "I have it! Now, for the game I have in mind, everyone must place their hands upon the table."

The Duke led the way, placing his two large hands on the table, palms down. Rapidly, the rest of the hall emulated him, the guests looking from one to another in amused anticipation of the game to follow.

"Now... Sir Wilbur!" Edgar called across the table to one of his close friends, "Kindly take one hand off the table and reach into the pocket of Sir Humphrey there beside you, and see what you can steal from him!"

The guests began to laugh at the direction the game was taking. Sir Wilbur's hand reached into his friend's pocket and produced a tobacco pouch. A cheer went up around the room as he held it up for all to see.

"Now you, Humphrey!" Edgar laughed, "What is in your neighbour's pocket?"

And so the game continued along the table. Tobacco, pipes, herbs, potions and kerchiefs appeared from the pockets of gentlemen and ladies.

"What! Are you all so sick in Oxford that you carry potions?" the Duke frowned as he pulled a vial of elixir from the pocket of Dean Mansfield.

"The air in town is pestilential, my lord," said

John by his side. "It is true that many are sick as a result."

"Well, you'll find no such thing in *my* pocket, young Scholar! Game on, game on – it is your turn."

John de Courcy reached tentatively into the Duke's pocket, more than a little apprehensive of what he might find. He felt a soft leather pouch and the hall roared with amusement as he pulled out a bag of coins.

"My money, you scoundrel!" the Duke shouted over the noise. "Edgar, I trust that your game is only a game – I've already given this man thirty sovereigns today!"

"Of course it is only for jest, sire," Edgar smiled. "De Courcy, put it down! Now, Miss Mansfield – it is your turn..."

Jane's hand moved under the table to a chorus of whistles around the room. She smiled as her fingers felt inside John's pocket, but then her brow furrowed and she turned to look at him, her eyes suddenly anxious as she opened her hand to reveal an object that brilliantly reflected the light of the thousand candles: a luminous gold and emerald ring.

V

John de Courcy stood nervously in an ante-chamber of the banqueting hall, guarded by two of the University bailiffs. Dean Mansfield sat in a heavy, wooden chair, while old Macebius, John's tutor, kept to his feet. Edgar lounged against the wall, looking disinterested in the whole scene. Harry Hopetoun had entered quietly and stood half hidden by the curtain.

The Duke burst angrily into the room and began pacing up and down like some kind of predatory animal. No one spoke as a servant offered wine to all except John, and then left the room. The Duke stopped pacing, drank deeply from the goblet and swallowed.

"So, de Courcy?" he roared. "Have you nothing to say?"

"My lord, I do not know what to say. Apart from seeing the ring upon your hand, I have neither seen nor touched it at any time. I swear it."

"And yet it is found within your pocket, on your person. Ha!" This was a different Duke to the one that John had known. This Duke was a soldier who thought nothing of killing, a merciless man of iron.

"I do maintain that, my lord, upon my honour!"

"Your *honour*, sir, has no great value at the moment."

Wise Old Macebius cleared his throat, saying "If I may speak, my lord. I know this man and would like to say something."

The Duke nodded. "As you will. I do not know how to proceed except to prison."

Macebius spoke firmly, undaunted by the grandeur of the Duke. He had seen dukes before, and princes, and knew them to be men like any other in the eyes of God.

"Firstly, as I said, I know John de Courcy to be an honest man. Second, and more important, he is in no way an idiot. Only an idiot would steal a precious ring and then carry it upon his person while he sits dining with the owner of that ring. Thirdly, he has no motive: today is the culmination of years of work for him, and he gained more by your patronage than he would gain by stealing the ring. Whatever the truth is of this matter, John de

Courcy is the victim of a crime, not the perpetrator."

"Yet I say he had both opportunity *and* motive," Edgar spat venom from his tongue. He would not miss this chance to see his rival defeated. "Was it not de Courcy who happened to be by your lordship when you fell from your horse this afternoon? He could easily have taken the ring while you were senseless. As for why: he is a poor man of no fortune, in love with a lady beyond his means. We all know a man would do anything for love, is that not so, de Courcy?"

Edgar's lips quivered in a victorious smile as he soaked in John's discomfort in front of Jane's father.

While John stood in the centre of the room, the Duke circled him like a wolf sizing up his prey. At last he stopped, standing face to face with him.

"I have an idea, de Courcy. I have listened to your Master Macebius. I know him to be a sensible man, and I know that you are famed as an honest man. But even honest men can be tempted. You had an opportunity to steal the ring and it was found upon your person. This does not look good, to any eyes.

But let us play a game of logic, as you academic men so like to play. Let us presume you are honest, as he says. Then you must *prove* that honesty. He says you are intelligent. Well then, I will give you five days of freedom – until Christmas – in which to use that intelligence to prove your innocence and deliver me the real criminal. If you are intelligent enough to be my Scholar, you will succeed. But if you fail, I will be without pity – for, in that case, either you are the thief or you have not the intelligence I hoped. Your punishment shall be gaol and ignominy. Do you accept my challenge?"

Master Macebius shook his head. John's face was grey with shock.

"I have no choice sir."

"Come, come. You can do better than that." the Duke retorted, "Be a man! You de Courcys may be honest, but we must teach you some spirit. If you are innocent, as old Macebius says you must be, then *fight* for that innocence, sir!"

"Yes, sir. I will, sir."

"Good, then I will see you in the great Hall five days hence."

Chapter 3

I

BACK IN HIS ROOM, John sat down heavily in the chair and put his head in his hands while Harry lit the candles and saw to the fire.

Tom, the mute servant boy, came in carrying a basket of wood for the fire in one hand and a pitcher of hot herbal infusion in the other. He could not speak, but his questioning eyes sufficed to ask why the two friends were not celebrating. Tom gestured to Harry, who told him what John had been accused of stealing. Tom's eyes opened so wide that they looked like they might fall out of his head, soon replaced by anger as he shook his head violently and gestured that this was not true!

"We know that, Tom, but the real criminal was clever to make it look as if John were the villain."

Tom took over from Harry at the fire and soon had it burning furiously. Then he poured two cups of his hot potion and gave one to each of the friends. John looked up and took the cup.

"You are a good man, Tom. Your special infusion was never so needed as tonight. Will you take one yourself? It is a cold night."

But before Tom could answer a shout rang out in to the night.

"Boy! Where are you, you mute idiot?" the voice echoed up the staircase. Tom shrugged sadly and gestured that he had to go, and ran from the room.

Harry shut the door behind him. The two friends looked at each other.

"And so even if the Duke does half-believe in my innocence, he would have me prove it or–"

He was interrupted by three gentle, but urgent knocks upon the door. Harry opened the door to reveal a boy standing in the darkness of the hall.

"What is it, boy?"

"May I come in, sir? I cannot talk out here."

Harry moved aside to let the boy enter.

"Well, what is it?"

"I came as soon as I heard, to see what service I could be."

"Who are you, boy? What on earth service could *you* be?"

"Don't you recognise me, Harry?"

Harry frowned at him, thinking there was something vaguely familiar about the boy but quite unable to say where he'd seen him before.

"I am afraid you have me at a loss, boy." he confessed.

"I'm not a boy, Harry." came the answer, "It is me: *Maude!*"

"Maude Mansfield! What in God's name are you doing dressed in this manner? And what would happen if people discovered you in a man's room at this hour – or at any hour for that matter?"

"I suppose you would have to marry me to save my honour, Harry. So there we are – I am risking *that* terrible fate in order to be of what service I can to your friend."

John smiled as Harry frowned and Maude sat down on the footstool near the fire.

"Miss Mansfield, your family never ceases to amaze me," he said. "Does your sister know of this?"

"A little. She is happier to obey the rules that govern young women than I am. This is the only way I am able to see a little more of the world and its ways. I see much, John, and that is where I hope to be of some help."

"Right now I need all the help I can get." John laughed.

II

"Good," Maude continued, "now all of us in this room know that you are innocent, John. Who else is on our side?"

"Macebius. He is certain of me."

"Hurrah for old Macebius. He is the best of men. What of you, Harry?"

"I don't understand. What do you mean?" Harry answered.

"You profess to be a supporter of the Queen, Harry, but your family's religious sympathies are well known. Maybe *you* are the one who wants to sabotage John's hopes and put a Catholic as the Duke's Scholar?"

Harry studied Maude with his head on one side, trying to judge whether she was joking or not. He could not be sure. Then he noticed that John was staring at him.

"For Christ's sake, man!" Harry exploded, "You are worth more to me than life itself!"

"More than eternal damnation?" Maude's eyes narrowed.

"Maude – stop this immediately! I am John's closest friend and would give my life for him. That is enough!"

Maude's expression relaxed and she smiled.

"I know."

"Maude, you are a cruel interrogator – *you* should be the one studying law, not me."

"Sadly, that is not possible in this world," she sighed. "My point is that you are the victim of a plot, John, so we must be careful what we say and who we trust."

"But who do we suspect?" John asked.

She looked at him with the beginnings of exasperation, but managed to control her expression.

"For an intelligent man, John, you are most unworldly. As the Duke's Scholar, you are to be adviser to one of the most important men in England. Tell me, what do you and your family stand for?"

"Honour... justice, truth... Elizabeth– "

"Exactly: Elizabeth. She is Queen to you and me, John, but to many others – even to some within this college – she is a usurper, the bastard child of a whore and a madman, and a blasphemous servant of the devil! The de Courcy family has a reputation for honour and decency, and their support for the Queen is well known – so it serves the Queen's enemies' purposes to see *you* discredited, John. These people hate you!"

There was a silence after this speech.

"Now – who had the opportunity to place that ring in your pocket, John?" Maude asked eventually.

"Jane was sitting next to me at dinner – but obviously it was not her."

"How do you know?" asked Maude.

The two friends looked at Maude in astonishment.

"I'm joking, gentlemen! Of course it wasn't Jane. But who was it?"

"My waistcoat was hanging in my room all day – someone could have put it there during the afternoon. And then Edgar and his friends attacked me on the way to the banquet, but although he has no love for me, he is a gentleman. I do not think he would steal from his own uncle and place the ring in my pocket."

Maude raised her eyes to the ceiling, mumbling "Even if the other man was his rival in love, glory and eternal redemption? He is of *their* mind, John, don't you know that?"

"I have never heard him talk of such things."

"Of course he does not talk of his religious convictions in public: it is too dangerous! But if you interested yourself in the movements inside this college as I do – there is only so much needlework a girl can endure in a day – you would see how often Sir Edgar visits our lord Prelate and his followers. You might even hear their private conversations, if you knew where to hide."

"Maude! Do you listen at keyholes?"

"I do not need to. Having lived in this college

from childhood, I know more of its secret ways and passages than most."

"Maude – we cannot accuse the Duke's *nephew*!" Harry interrupted, "Not without absolute, incontrovertible proof."

"True. So let us find it." she retorted calmly, "What do we know of the Duke's movements after he fell from his horse, for instance? Do we know what he did in the afternoon, before he found the ring had gone?"

The two friends' eyes opened in alarm and they avoided Maude's clear gaze.

"John? Harry? Tell me!"

John cleared his throat.

"After I was accused, we did question the Duke in private about his activities this afternoon, Maude." he explained, "It is not suitable for a young lady's ears. Nor even a young boy's ears."

"Why, was he engaged in some bawdy business?"

The friends' eyes opened even wider than before.

"Now, now. Do not look so surprised. We women are not as naïve as you would like to think us. Why, it is said that in Eastern countries the Mamas bring the courtesans to their daughters before they are married to teach them the ways of such things."

Harry guffawed with laughter, his eyes shining with amusement. John cleared his throat.

"Well, then – yes – the Duke was engaged in 'bawdy business' as you put it."

"All afternoon?"

"All afternoon."

"She must have been exhausted."

"There were two of them."

Maude put her hand over her mouth and giggled quietly.

"Do we know their names?"

"No – the Duke had no idea what they were called because they were procured for him by Edgar. He could only tell us that one had dark hair and the other was blonde. However, he searched them intimately and is satisfied that they did not have the ring."

"And no one else came or went from the room?"

"No one. Tom came with wine and cakes, but

he did not enter the room. And Tom is as honest as you or I. He would not take anything from anyone. If it had been any other servant maybe, but we know that Tom is not a thief."

The trio nodded in agreement and were then once again silent as they looked for a way forward where they could find no obvious path.

III

Emilie Banter climbed the stairs to her room in the small hours of the morning. Her legs felt like stone. It had been a long and difficult day. Edgar had got her out of her bed long before midday to service the Duke, who had proved a rough master. And then there were the further demands of Edgar himself later in the later evening. Although he had employed her for the Duke, Edgar had been jealous of his uncle and so had demanded her attention this same night.

Emilie smiled to herself and shivered. She had done all Edgar had asked of her – and more. And in return she would soon be Lady Hardridge. At this thought, she began to ascend the stairs with renewed energy and soon reached her room at the top of the building.

Lady Hardridge! And maybe she could take her friend Meg with her as her serving maid, so they could both get away from this life and live as honest women! Soon she would be married. Maybe before the New Year. And then life would be different.

Emilie turned the handle, pushed open the door to her rooms and went in. Over the familiar scent of perfume she detected another, unfamiliar smell. She lit a candle and lost her breath as it illuminated a dark figure sitting in the chair.

"Good evening, Miss Banter. I trust you are well?"

"You startled me, sir. What will you at this late hour? And what do you mean by entering my room, sir? I need to go to my bed."

"Simply a talk, Emilie. I have something I would like to discuss with you. Look I have poured you some wine." The man held out a goblet towards her.

Chapter 4

I

THE SHORTEST DAY OF THE YEAR dawned drowned in fog. The fog crawled up from the three rivers that surrounded Oxford and made an island of the town. It made its way into every crack and opening, so even the rooms were foggy.

John turned left off the High Street down the Turl. Following some directions that he had been given by old Macebius that morning, he arrived at the house of a certain Mrs. Munsby. He looked up at the half-timbered façade disappearing in to the fog. Someone shouted a warning from above, and John just had time to press himself against the building before the contents of a basin landed where he had just been standing. As the liquid splashed across the street, he was reassured to see that it was simply washing water, not something worse.

He ran his fingers through his hair, looked up and down the street to make sure no one was watching him, and knocked on the door. After some considerable time he heard footsteps and a key turning in the lock.

"Well, young man?" a woman said as she opened the door, "Isn't it a bit early in the day to be coming here?"

John blushed with embarrassment.

"Oh, excuse me, mistress. I am not here for... on business. I mean I *am* here on business but not the sort – I mean – not *your* business."

"Well, if it's not my business then what in hell's name are you doing waking my girls when the sun is not even up?" The woman opened the door a little more and peered up at the fog. Her face was old and tired, but her hair was a vibrant shade of red, as was her robe.

"I come to talk to Mrs. Munsby. Master Macebius of Christ Church sent me."

"Ah!" she smiled, opening the door fully. "You

must come in then. Macebius is a good gentleman, and if he sent you to me then I am sure you are too. Come in, come in – don't let all the cold in with you."

John followed the large woman in her sumptuous red robe along a dark corridor and into a large room. He had never before seen such a room: there were divans and soft seats, all in velvets and brocade, and luxuriously-cushioned alcoves. The pictures on the walls made John's eyes open in amazement for they depicted ancient scenes of nymphs and shepherds – as one would expect in a classical painting – but doing extraordinary things to each other, in positions that made John blush once again.

Mrs. Munsby followed the direction of John's gaze.

"I can see you're not accustomed to bawdy houses, young man. Your name?"

"John, madam, John de Courcy."

Mrs. Munsby's hand flew to her mouth.

"Oh, my poor lamb! It's you!" She looked closely at him. "But you don't look like a thief. Is it true? Are you the villain they say?"

"How is it you have heard of me?"

"It was all the talk of the town last night, lad: the new Scholar stealing the Duke's ring and then being discovered by the lady he loves in front of everyone at the banquet! But tell me, is it true?"

"Some is true. I am the Duke's scholar, and the lost ring was found in my pocket by... by a lady. But I am not the villain that stole it, Mrs. Munsby. I am the victim of a plot against me."

Mrs. Munsby peered again at John.

"Aye, I think you speak truly. And I heard as much from many others last night. And so why does Macebius send you to me? To raise your spirits? I perceive by your look that you have never been with a lady such as my girls. No – nor any lady – I can see it in your blush, but surely this is not the time to..."

"No, madam. That is not why I am here! I am in need of information, and Macebius thought that you might be able to help me."

"I will do what I can, lad."

"I need to know, Mrs. Munsby, which women they were that spent yesterday afternoon with the Duke in his chamber?"

Mrs. Munsby pursed her lips and thought a moment.

"None of my girls, I can say clearly. Some of them do a little afternoon work now and then, but they were all here yesterday. It was so cold, we were all sat around the fire, mending our clothes. Can you describe these two women? I know most of the bawdy girls around the town, so they may be familiar to me."

"Only that they are young, that one is blonde and the other dark, and that they are... well proportioned," John lifted his hands helplessly. "The Duke commented that they were in good condition as regards their teeth and all that."

Mrs. Munsby raised her eyes to the heavens.

"Lord above! You would think that the Duke was talking about his horses, not girls. Still, that is the business we are in. And do you know how the Duke procured these girls – I presume he did not go to the bawdy house and find them himself?"

"They were procured by Sir Edgar Hardridge, a young relative of–"

Mrs. Munsby's face had clouded over.

"I know who Sir Edgar is, as do most of the

women in this town. And never a surer villain did I see than he."

"He is not an entirely good man, I know. Indeed I have had many troubles with him myself, but he is a noble – and a gentleman."

"He is no *gentleman*, sir," she answered. "I do not know a madam in this town who would accept him in her house. He must have found his girls on the streets, sir, girls who operate alone. There is such a girl with hair as you describe, who is often seen with Edgar – Emilie, she is called. Emilie Banter. At this hour she will still be in her bed – turn left at the end of the alley, and look for a door with a lion's head over it. Her room is at the top of the stairs."

John got slowly to his feet from the soft chair he had been sat in and thanked Mrs. Munsby for her time.

"Don't speak of it, sir. There are not many honest men in this town – if you are truly one of them, as you seem, I am happy to help you. And when your troubles are resolved, and you are free to claim your lady love, you are welcome to come again – free of charge, sir. There are things a young man should know before he marries, sir, and I have some nice clean girls who would be glad to give you a lesson."

II

The fog was lifting a little as John emerged from the door of Mrs. Munsby's house. He turned down the alley as she had said and found the house with the lion's head above the door. He climbed up the narrow wooden stairs, and knocked on the door at the top. There was no answer. He knocked again. Nothing.

He tried the door and, finding it unlocked, he entered. The decor of the room and the bed reminded him of Mrs. Munsby's house, but nobody was home. John went forward and put his hand between the bedsheets. They were stone cold. No one had slept here this night. He frowned and looked about the room. On the table there were papers, ink and quill, which made him frown deeper. He picked up one of the papers and read:

"My dearest love, my heart beats fast at thinking of your..."

There was no more. The message was written in a naïve but able hand. It was not scholarly writing, but this woman had some education. John tore off a section of the paper and wrote upon it. Then he left his note in plain view for her to see when she returned and went out into the street again.

III

As John came out on to the street, a woman leaning in the doorway two houses along called softly out to him.

"If she is not able to fulfil your desires, sir, maybe one of the girls here could?"

John approached the woman and looked her up and down.

"Is this a bawdy house, Madam?"

"Lord! You are a serious young man, aren't you? Some might call it that."

"Do you know anything of Emilie Banter who lives in that house there? I need to talk to her on a matter of urgency, but she is not home."

The woman shrugged her shoulders.

"It is not like Miss Emilie to be out at this hour

of the day. She never normally rises before noon. But come in, sir. I will call for her friend, Meg, who may be able to help you. They are often out together, so she may know where Emilie is."

The woman beckoned John in to a room similar to Mrs. Munsby's but dirtier and darker, with torn and stained furnishings. "*Good God,*" thought John, "*I have never been in a bawdy house in all my life and now in one morning I have entered two and a whore's bedroom.*"

The woman reappeared with a very attractive girl, not more than twenty years old, wrapped in a heavy blanket against the cold. The girl's long dark hair was a mess and she yawned widely.

"Today of all days, after such a tiring day as yesterday, I have a morning visitor," she sighed. The girl sat down opposite John and stared belligerently at him. "Well sir – have you got me out of my bed to stare at me?"

John cleared his throat.

"No – I am here on a matter of business. I am looking for a girl who might have been with the Duke of Gloucester yesterday afternoon."

The girl's expression flickered for barely a moment.

"And why are you talking to me about it?"

"The description of one of the girls fits that of Emilie Banter, and she is apparently... friends with Sir Edgar Hardridge, who I know procured the girls for the Duke."

"And what is this to you, sir? Are you a Constable for the Duchess?"

"No, miss, I am falsely accused of stealing the Duke's ring and face gaol if I cannot discover the truth. I am hoping this Emilie Banter might be able to help."

"So you are John de Courcy?" she said, eyeing John up and down in a new light. "And why should she be able to help?" the girl glanced sideways to where the older woman listened intently while pretending to concentrate on mending a hole in a stocking.

"I need to know if Emilie or the other girl have any knowledge of the ring and when it went missing. I have only a few short days before I am thrown in gaol and all my life ruined."

The girl frowned and again glanced quickly at the woman in the corner of the room.

"I am indeed a friend of Emilie Banter, sir. But I know not where she is if she is not in bed. When she returns I will ask her to come to you, if you will tell me where she should look?"

"She can leave a message for me at the gate of Christ Church College."

"Will that not look a little strange to the guards that keep the gate, sir?"

"You are kind to think of such things, Miss...?"

"Marber. Meg Marber."

"–but I am beyond caring about my reputation as a virtuous man," said John, rising to his feet. "It is my very life I am fighting for."

Meg stood up as John did, and led him back to the front door.

"A foggy day, sir!" she said, a little too loud, then whispered, "Meet me by Hargrave the Butcher's in the market at 4 o'clock. Now go."

The other woman appeared suddenly behind Meg, who touched her long dark curls and tried to look nonchalant as the woman stared hard at her.

"Whose side are you on, you hussy?"

"What do you take me for? A fool? I have to dress. I need to have words with someone," and Meg flounced off.

IV

John came in to his rooms to find Harry already sitting there, eating some lunch that Tom had recently provided for them. Seeing the food John realised how hungry he was and, pulling a chair to the table, he grasped bread, cheese, butter, pickled fruits, and started to eat.

"Well?" said Harry through a mouthful of food.

John wished to concentrate on eating a little more before answering.

"You first, Harry – what did you find out from the servants and stable boys?"

"Well, the stable boys are not a talkative crowd, but I suppose a life of cleaning up horse shit does not encourage conversation. I did find one helpful chap called Brane – an ironic name, as I don't think he has much intelligence. He says that the Duke needed help dismounting from his horse because of his injury, and so he ordered Brane and another boy to form a sort of human pedestal for him. Brane swears that he felt a ring press into the skin of his shoulder as the Duke dismounted, and that he looked and saw the emerald, there upon the Duke's finger."

"And he will testify this?"

"He will, although if anyone cross-questions him too vigorously, John, I do not know how good he will be under pressure. He is a simple young man."

"There is no one else?"

"Not among the other stable boys. They said nothing, although I suspect that some of them knew more than they were admitting. Maybe someone has commanded them to be silent, but forgot about the simple Brane."

"And the servants?"

"The kitchen servants were more inclined to talk. In fact, it was quite difficult to get away from them. They all have theories about whether you are guilty or not, and who else might have done the crime! But they did confirm that the Duke asked for wine and cakes, and that it was indeed Tom, and only Tom, who went to the Duke's room."

"And what of your papist brothers, Harry? What did they have to say about me?"

"Very funny I'm sure, de Courcy. My 'papist brothers' as you call them, were very kind about you. I didn't hear a bad word. They are all as mystified as we are."

"Or acting."

"There is that... and there is no sign of Edgar. He has disappeared."

John contemplated this in silence.

"And what of your morning, John?" Harry lifted an amused eyebrow at his friend. "Did you find your house of ill-repute in the fog?"

"I think I may say that I am now more of a man of the world than I was before, Harry. Having never set foot inside a bawdy house I have now entered two of the places and encountered some interesting women along the way. You will meet one of them later – a pretty, dark-haired girl called Meg, who has given us a *rendez-vous* by Hargrave the Butcher when the market closes at four o'clock. She has information about Emilie

Banter, who may be the blonde girl we're looking for. They are friends."

"And this Meg is dark haired – is she then the other girl?"

John looked thoughtful and slightly dismayed.

"I do not think a lovely young girl like that could consort with an old man like the Duke?"

"Of course she could, John: to eat, to have clothes, a roof over her head, and some cheap jewels to lighten her life a little?"

John's eyes were filled with sadness at Harry's words and he nodded slowly.

"You are right. I was naïve to say such a thing."

"Naïve, but also a little captivated, I think, by this dark-haired young woman. I look forward to meeting her."

Chapter 5

I

THE ONLY LIGHT came from a small window high up near the apex of the roof. When Emilie awoke, she could remember nothing and had no idea where she was. She looked around, and instantly felt the pain from injuries on her legs and body. She tried to move her arms but found they were tied behind her back with a cord.

What had happened? Why was she in this strange, cold place, and was she still in Oxford or somewhere else? Her head ached and there was a taste of something bitter and foul in her mouth.

Emilie tried to focus on the room. She could see that she was in an attic, the steep roof rising up above her head. She could hear the sounds of mice, or maybe something bigger, all around her. She began to cry, but bit her lip to stop herself: Emilie Banter was not one for crying. She had been in trouble before and survived. This time would be no different.

At some point, she must have fallen unconscious again because it was night when she woke up. Someone was in the room, holding a candle. She saw a figure, hooded like an executioner, standing over her.

"Oh, don't worry. You're not going to die. We might even decide not to harm you again, who knows?" Emilie vaguely recognised the voice and the high-pitched laugh. "Here – eat this."

The figure pushed a tray of bread and cheese and a steaming mug towards her.

"My hands – I can't – "

"I will free one hand, whore, but the other one stays tied behind your back. And don't think of trying to escape – the door is locked. There's a bucket in the corner if you need to piss."

The man came closer so that Emilie could almost see his face in the candlelight as he cut the rope and released her right hand.

"Please – why am I here?" she asked.

"Some people want you out of the way for a few days. Don't worry. You will not be harmed – much – unless you make noise or try to escape."

The hooded figure laughed viciously and, taking the candle, lifted a trapdoor in the floor and disappeared down a ladder one step at a time, like a goblin descending to hell, until the door closed, a bolt was locked shut and Emilie was left in darkness.

She felt her way to the bread and cheese and drank the warm, spicy wine in the mug. She felt its warmth filling her chest and smiled in spite of her situation. After she had eaten and drunk and found her way across to the piss-bucket and back to the mattress, the weariness overcame her once more so that she could do nothing but lie down on the bedding and sleep.

II

Four dark-robed men were gathered in the room beneath Emilie's prison. The moisture of the fog had made the Prelate's face even more pustulent and tender. He looked up towards the trap-door in the ceiling and raised an eyebrow at the man who had recently come down from there.

"Is she awake, Croke?"

"No lord, she will be sleeping now. The Irish witch assured me that the herbs are strong. She will not wake for many hours."

"When this matter is resolved, remind me to investigate the Irish witch."

"The witch has been useful before, lord. Surely we do not want to lose her?"

"There'll always be another witch, fool! The streets of Oxford are full of witches and bawds. Thank the heavens for the sanctuary of the college. Now, what news of the de Courcy boy?"

"He can do nothing, lord. While the girl is imprisoned above us, there is no one that would betray us. She is his only chance and we have her secure."

"She will not start shouting for help up there? A woman's scream can penetrate the thickest walls."

"The herbs will keep her docile, lord. But maybe Sir Edgar should visit her – she is attached to him, and he has promised her marriage if she is good and keeps her silence."

The men all laughed at such an absurd idea. Even the Prelate, who was not given to frivolity, smiled pustulently. He turned to the man charged with guarding Emilie.

"A good idea. Tell Sir Edgar to visit her when she wakes and pacify her with his false promises. What of the second whore? She is watched?"

"She is followed everywhere she goes by one of our spies, lord."

"Good, good. And are your spies good men, Mr. Croke?"

"They are, lord. Very good men indeed."

Chapter 6

I

THE SOMBRE LIGHT was rapidly fading as John and Harry walked through the market, the merchants closing their stalls for the day. The dampness of the fog had penetrated everything and everyone in the town, and the market people moved with heads bent against the cold.

Harry and John found the stall of Hargrave the Butcher, but there was no sign of Meg in the crowd of people. The clock of nearby Exeter College gave four melancholy rings in the freezing afternoon air. John and Harry kept to the shadows and waited for the woman to appear.

When the college clock sounded a quarter

past four, the friends shifted from foot to foot and looked at each other anxiously.

"She was very firm about the time." John said, "I hope nothing has happened to her."

"Do you think we should stay? Once the light has gone, she will not be able to see us even if she comes."

"I know it is cold, Harry, but give her a few more minutes."

The friends walked up and down to keep themselves warm. Soon, the only light in the dark street came from the neighbouring taverns. Then John saw a figure in the crowd, walking quickly, the hood of her cloak pulled over the dark curls of her hair. He recognised Meg, but as she approached he could see from her expression that she was warning him not to speak to her. She looked back over her shoulder and pretended to bump in to John, dropping her cloth bag to the floor. They both bent to pick up the bag.

"I am followed. And Emilie Banter has disappeared. Meet me behind the Bear Tavern at two o'clock in the morning. Come alone. I'm frightened."

And she disappeared once more into the twilight.

John walked quickly over to where Harry stood blowing into his hands.

"Well, friend?" Harry asked. "Have we not waited long enough for your tardy madam?"

"We have, Harry. She was here. And Emilie has disappeared."

II

Emilie opened her eyes and looked about her. She remembered where she was, and could tell by the dim light that it was morning. The sun did not rise fully before nine o'clock at this time of year. She had slept for many hours.

She frowned and felt that same familiar metallic taste on her tongue. This was not right. She had never slept long, not even as a child. Why start now on this uncomfortable mattress in this cold attic with rats for company and bruises all over her body?

She remembered the hot infusion she had drunk down thirstily the night before. She looked through the half-light and moved across to where she had left the empty mug, scattering rats and mice as she did so. She sniffed it. Wine, cinnamon, cloves, nutmeg, apples – and something else – behind those other smells she could detect something else.

She heard a movement over by the trapdoor. A bar was drawn back and the door lifted in the floor. In the thin light she saw a familiar face appearing.

"Edgar! Oh Edgar, at last. You have come to rescue me!"

Edgar came up the ladder, placing a tray of food and drink on the floor, and shut the trapdoor behind him. Emilie threw herself in to his arms as best she could with one hand tied.

"Oh Edgar, I knew you would come for me! Untie me and let us get away from this place!"

Edgar took her free hand, led her back to the mattress and sat her down.

"Let's not go too fast, Emilie, my love. Did nobody tell you that you are here for your own safety? Your hand was tied so that you would not endanger yourself by trying to escape. It is very dangerous out in the streets at the moment. If the Duke were to find out that *you* took the ring, he will have you executed as a thief. We wouldn't want that, would we?"

Emilie looked at him, frowning.

"But I only took the ring on your command, Edgar. And you are his nephew, so you can tell him what happened. Besides, the Duke searched me from head to toe and found nothing, so he knows I am not the thief. But you could be. Anyone could be who was not searched that night. But not me–"

"All the same, suspicion has fallen on you."

"And Meg? Is she imprisoned also?"

"She is safe."

"But where?"

"Woman, be quiet! You ask too many questions."

"Edgar, this is not fair. I do as you say, for which I am hurt, captured and imprisoned in a cold, dark attic where I am..."

She paused for a moment. Something in Edgar's expression made her stop before she told him about the drug she had detected in her drink.

"...where I am forced to keep company with mice and rats..."

"Quiet, I said! You encounter more than a few rats in your line of work, I think?" Edgar laughed at his little joke.

Emilie looked at Edgar with a quizzical expression. She felt a cold, grey doubt enter her mind.

"You are not come to release me, Edgar?"

"It is for your own safety, love." Edgar, seeing the hard expression in her eyes, remembered how crucial her silence was for the time being, and moved towards her to kiss her neck, her face, her mouth. "When this business is over, we shall be together at last and you shall be Lady Hardridge. In a few short days, the villain de Courcy will be jailed, I will be made Duke's scholar in his place, and then all shall be well. I shall be able to pay all my debts – and yours – and we shall have a house to live in and money to live on."

Emilie sat back against the wooden pillar that supported the roof above their heads. Edgar took her free hand in his and kissed the butterfly tattoo on her wrist.

"We shall be free, like the butterfly, sweetheart..."

Edgar gave her one last passionate kiss and disappeared back down the ladder, bolting the door behind him.

Emilie carried her tray back to the mattress. She was thirsty, but sniffed at the mug of wine and put it back untouched on the tray, taking only the food. She sat for a long time, until she heard noise in the room below. Silently, she moved toward the trapdoor and put her ear to it.

"She is asleep?" a muffled voice asked.

"She will be – she was ravenous when I saw her, she will have eaten and drunk the wine an hour since."

Emilie's hand flew to her mouth as she recognised the voice of Edgar below.

"I do not like to take a human life, Edgar, but she must be silenced in order to restore God to his proper place in England. Our cause is greater than the life of a whore."

"Amen!"

Emilie shuddered as she heard several voices chorus approval for her death.

"Croke, you will go back to the witch to get a potion that will finish her. Can we trust the witch?"

"I think not, Lord. She has been discreet so far, but believes I only take the potion to help me sleep. I will ask her to mix me more, and take arsenic from her stocks while she prepares the potion."

"And you, Edgar Hardridge, we can trust you? You have had an understanding with the girl I believe?"

"She has been a useful and pleasant diversion, lord, but nothing more."

Emilie heard the men below. Had she ever really believed him? There had been men like him before, promises that turned to dust. But Edgar was such a handsome rogue. Yes, she had let herself believe him.

"Go and arrange the poison now, Croke. We will delay no further. When she awakes again, Edgar, you will take her some drugged wine. When she is unconscious, Croke will perform the last rites. The least we can do is ensure the girl goes to heaven eventually, although her stay in purgatory may be a long one."

III

John and Harry heard the night watch call two o'clock as they waited in the shadows behind the Bear Tavern. It was dangerous to be on the street at this hour. If the night watch discovered them, they might find themselves in gaol some days earlier than expected.

A door opened across the little square and a figure hurried towards them. John lifted an arm so that she could see he was there in the darkness.

"John de Courcy?"

"And my friend Harry."

"I can't stay long, I am watched wherever I go. That is why I could not talk this afternoon. Two girls are distracting the men who watch me, but they will notice my absence soon. Now listen, I did not tell you all. Emilie is gone."

"Gone?"

"We have a code, a way to tell the other when we are on a job. It is dangerous work that girls like us do, gentlemen, and we need to protect each other. She is gone, and she has left no sign in her room as arranged."

"What can we do?"

"If you value your freedom, sir, you must find Emilie. I was with her that afternoon with the Duke, sir. She asked me to come. But there was more to it than she told me. I don't know the details, but Emilie hopes to marry, you see, and I know she would do anything for a decent marriage..."

"Marriage!"

"Yes, sir, marriage. And what is so strange about that? There are many ladies and duchesses that did not start out so fine in life, sir. A young man's head is easily turned by a pretty girl. But there was something Emilie did not tell me about the business with the Duke. I can tell when she is keeping something from me."

"The ring?"

"It's not impossible. The Duke searched me so thoroughly that I still have the marks, but he was gentler with Emilie. They always are with blondes, sir, as if they are more fragile than us dark-haired maidens. All I know is that if you find Emilie, you will find some answers."

"What of you, Meg?" John asked, "Are you safe?"

"I don't know, sir. I'm so scared. These men follow me everywhere. If only I could find somewhere safe..." Meg let the end of her sentence fade away.

"Would you come with us? Now?"

"*John?*"

"*Shh*, Harry!"

"But, John – where shall we take her to?" Harry insisted, "We are not allowed women in the colleges–"

"She is a witness, Harry. If we want to keep her safe, then we must take her with us. She can stay in my room – Tom will not tell anyone."

"Do you mean, sir...?" Meg asked doubtfully.

"No, Meg, I am not that sort of a man. I am offering you sanctuary, that is all, until we find Emilie and sort this business out."

"Then I will come, sir!"

"John!" Harry protested.

"Oh shut up, Harry! I thought you were the adventurous one of us two."

IV

As John led Meg and Harry quietly into his rooms, he jumped in shock to discover Maude, dressed as a boy again, sitting in his chair.

"Maude! For the love of God! You made me jump out of my skin."

Maude, too, jumped in surprise as she saw Meg enter the room behind the two men.

"I'm so sorry, gentlemen," she said angrily, "I didn't realise I was interrupting an illicit party."

Meg raised her eyebrows disdainfully at Maude, who returned the look.

"Don't be silly, Maude," said Harry, "This is Meg – she needs our protection."

"Maude?" said Meg archly. "You are not, then, a young boy? But you make such a convincing one."

The two females stared at one another in mutual antagonism.

"Meg was... in the chamber with the Duke on the afternoon the ring disappeared, Maude." Harry explained, "We have brought her here to keep her safe while we look for Emilie Banter. That is the name of the other girl."

"Emilie – the blonde one, with the butterfly tattoo?"

"How do you know these things Maude?" Harry frowned.

"Eyes and ears, Harry, that's all." Maude smiled innocently at him, while Meg narrowed her eyes at her.

"So how do we find this Emilie?" Maude asked, looking from one friend to the other, expectantly.

"There are places I know where she may be hiding." Meg suggested, "I will tell you where to–"

"Why don't you start by questioning Edgar, John?" Maude interrupted her.

John looked from one woman to the other, clearly troubled by their competing demands.

"We can talk to Edgar in the morning," he decided. "First, I think we should listen to Meg's suggestions."

"I see. Obviously you don't need my help if you have hers. Fools!" Maude jumped to her feet and marched out of the room, slamming the door behind her.

Chapter 7

I

JOHN AND HARRY searched for Emilie Banter all over Oxford that night, looking in all the places that Meg suggested, but without success. The next morning, tired and dejected, they asked Master Macebius to summon Edgar Hardridge to his rooms so that John might question him. Harry waited secretly outside, ready to follow Edgar when he exited Macebius' rooms and see where he went next.

To his surprise, Edgar came out of Macebius' rooms much sooner than he had expected. Harry retreated into an alcove as Edgar passed by him, and then followed discreetly. To his surprise, Edgar did not exit the college itself, but walked in the direction of the Chapel.

Harry entered the Chapel some seconds after Edgar, just in time to see him disappear into the priest's rooms. Harry could not follow, but listened at the door. He could hear the voices of several men, but could make out no words. There was a moment of silence. Then, suddenly, the men began to shout: a door slammed shut and he heard footsteps coming his way. Harry just had time to hide behind a tapestry before the door opened and the men came out into the chapel.

"Find the whore! She cannot have got far!" he heard Edgar say. "She must have escaped across the roof..."

"The whore's a monkey, to climb up there!"

"Get our men on to the roofs. There is no escape for her that way. Make sure she falls and then there will be no need for poison! Come – alert the guards!"

The steps receded and Harry came out from behind the tapestry. No one was there. He left the chapel and joined a crowd of students who had been alerted by the cries and were looking excitedly up at the roof.

Guards soon appeared on the roof, nervously moving on hands and knees across the wet tiles, accompanied by the excited shouts of the students below. The search continued without success and Harry finally decided that the woman must have made her escape, so he returned to Macebius's rooms to hear what John had learned from Edgar.

As he entered, he saw to his surprise that John was unconscious, his head resting on the table.

"Drugged." Macebius explained, coming to stand by him. "Hardridge will deny it, of course, and say that it was my own wine we drank, but he must have put a sleeping potion in John's goblet."

The door flew open and Maude came in, panting for breath.

"Did you see that excitement on the roof, Macebius? What fun! And all for nothing – there was not a sign of her! What's happened to John? Is he *asleep*?

"Drugged. By Hardridge." Harry explained.

Maude giggled.

"How can you laugh?"

"I am sorry, Harry. It seems I can do nothing without angering you. Well, Master Macebius, did Sir Edgar say anything of use?"

"Nothing," sighed Macebius. "The villain must have drugged the wine, because John was unconscious soon after he drank it. He will be asleep for hours now, so you must continue without him, Harry. Time is short."

"But now we have no idea where to look for Emilie Banter, if it was she who escaped over the roof."

"True. I suggest a new tactic: speak to those in Oxford who might have supplied Edgar with a sleeping potion." He handed Harry a piece of parchment upon which he had been writing, "These are the witches and potion-makers that I am familiar with – see if any of them will talk to you."

"Maude, will you stay with John?" Harry suggested.

"John will have Master Macebius with him," she replied, "I am going to keep looking for Emilie."

"If she escaped over the roof she might be anywhere!" Harry protested.

"Indeed so." Maude agreed, "*If* she escaped over the roof."

"What do you mean?"

"As I said before, Harry, if you ever paid me the courtesy of listening, I passed half my childhood in exploration of this college," she said, turning to leave the room, "I am familiar with passages that are a secret even to his holiness, the pustulent Prelate."

II

Emilie Banter lay in the dark. She was cold, and her wrist was bleeding from the friction of freeing her hand from the cord. Her fingers were cut from the effort of pulling away a section of the plaster wall in the attic, creating a hole just big enough for her to escape from her prison into the next section of the college's attic.

Before she left, she had opened the skylight to give her captors the impression that she had escaped onto the roof. After going through the wall, she had pulled a box in front of it to hide the hole. She was now in a space with no window and no light. She had drunk nothing for more than a day. Cold and too afraid to move, she thought that she might die here. The cold would take her quite quickly. She let her eyes close, wanting only to sleep...

"Emilie!"

She awoke with a start. She was still in darkness.

"Emilie!" The voice was very quiet, that of a girl.

Emilie lay very still, her mind racing. She did not recognise this voice.

"Emilie! If you are in here – do not be afraid. I am a friend. I have come to help. Are you here?"

"I am." The words were out of Emilie's mouth before she could stop them.

"Emilie! Where are you? Do not move – I will come to you."

"Over here."

"I am coming. I cannot light a torch as the flame will set the college on fire, but I can show you the way out of here."

Emilie let out an involuntary cry as she felt a hand upon her shoulder. The person felt down her arm to take her hand.

"Come – we must be absolutely silent or they will hear us below."

The two figures moved slowly along one of the roof timbers. When they got to the next wall, Emilie was taken through another small opening, similar to the one through which she had escaped from her prison room. In this part of the vast attic, there was a small window in the roof, letting through a little light.

"Holy God in Heaven, what have they done to you!" gasped Maude.

Emilie peered at her saviour and was surprised to see a familiar young boy, rather than a girl. She had seen him around town.

"Don't I know you, boy?"

"I am a girl. It is only the suit that is male, and the heart at times. And yes – you might have seen me in this guise once or twice. Now, *shhh!* We are above the banquet hall. Do you see that door across there? That is our destination. But we must be extra careful not to make a sound as we cross."

The two girls smiled at each other and Maude squeezed Emilie's unwounded hand.

"Come on. We are nearly there. You will be safe soon."

The two girls once more stepped gracefully along the timbers. In the enormous hall beneath their feet, oblivious students sat eating, while the two girls, both filthy from head to foot, balanced on the roof beams.

They reached the small, wooden door. Beyond this there were more attics and yet more. Finally they passed into an attic that was very different to the others: the floor was laid with planks, and large skylights let in plenty of light. The room contained tables and chairs, benches, tapestries, chests and vast paintings.

"This is my favourite place in the college. I come here often. Look–"

Maude gestured towards an area where a carpet and cushions had been laid out upon the floor. A small bookshelf full of books sat to one side. A number of candle-holders sat upon the bookshelf, with half-burnt candles in them, unlit.

"You must not tell a soul. No one ever comes up here. I don't think anyone even knows this place exists."

"It is very nice."

"It is cold and there is no fire, but it is warmed a little by my room below and there are many cloths you can wrap yourself in. The stairs go down to my chamber, and the door is hidden behind a tapestry that has been there since before my family came to Christ Church. I only found the door because I was hiding from my nurse one day. She never found me."

Maude laughed quietly.

"Who are you?"

"I am Maude Mansfield, daughter of the Dean of this college. There are no ladies in the college, as you know, but an exception was made for us because the Queen wanted our father to be Dean. I have been travelling these attics since I was a child. When Edgar's men went searching for you on the roof, it was clear where they had been keeping you prisoner. I guessed how you had escaped and where I might be able to find you."

"I am forever in your debt, Maude Mansfield. But what do we do now?"

"Firstly, I will bring you water and clean

clothes. And food! Lord! You must be starving and thirsty! Stay. I will return."

And Maude was gone down the staircase. Emilie stood staring after her smiling and wondering that such a high-born young lady should take the Lord's name in vain almost as much as a bawd.

III

Meg walked to and fro in the confines of John de Courcy's chamber. No one had been near the room for hours. She was cold, hungry and angry. A noise at the outer door made her hide behind the heavy curtains on either side of the window. She heard the door to the chamber open and there was the sound of something being dragged across the floor. She dared to look out and saw Harry Hopetoun and the servant boy, Tom, dropping John de Courcy on to the bed where he lay motionless.

"Is he dead?" asked Meg.

Tom's eyes opened wide as he saw a pretty young woman peering out from behind the curtain.

"Drugged. Your friend Edgar Hardridge spiked his wine."

"Sir Edgar?"

"The same, and we do not know how long it will last. I found the witch who provided the potion – she said it could be anything up to a day and a night, depending on the dose given."

"You visited a *witch*?" Meg's eyes were wide with fear. "Which witch?"

"I visited quite a number of witches, as a matter of fact, but the one in question was a pleasant Irish woman on Paradise Street."

"Mrs. O'Flaherty?"

"Yes – you know her?"

Meg recollected herself, arranged her expression and shrugged nonchalantly. "No, of course not, but I know *of* her. All the girls do. She provides help when they are – well – in trouble."

Harry winced at the thought.

"It is she who is in trouble now. She is convinced that her family is in danger due to all this business. And she is probably right: our enemies will stop at nothing. Have you heard about the woman on the roof?" he asked.

"How do you expect me to hear any news? I have seen no one, done nothing, had nothing to eat or drink..." Meg was once again the girl in charge.

"My apologies. John was supposed to take care of that. Tom, go and find food and drink for this lady. Not a word to anyone, do you understand?"

As Tom disappeared from the room, glancing strangely at Meg as he went, Harry turned to find Meg staring at him in a curious fashion.

"What is it? Why are you looking at me like that?"

"You called me a lady. No one ever calls me a lady." She moved closer to Harry and stroked his cheek with her finger.

Harry blushed hotly and mumbled something, just as Maude flew through the door and, seeing the two so close to each other, came to an abrupt halt, her mouth open and her eyes wide.

Harry, caught red-handed by Maude, looked crossly at her, "What? What do you want now? And what do you mean by bursting in to people's rooms like this?"

"I– I–" Maude looked at Harry with hurt

incomprehension, the excitement in her face deflated before she turned briskly around and ran out again.

"Maude!" Harry called angrily after her.

"Shhh!" said Meg, taking one of his hands in hers. "You are not meant to have females here! Let her go. Come, tell me your news, Harry. Was this lady on the roof Emilie?"

"We do not know for certain," said Harry wearily, "but if it was, then she was so close! Now she is gone and no one knows where. I must leave you and go out again among the streets and taverns to see if there is any sign of her."

"I will help you again, Harry," Meg said, "there are other places I have thought of where she might go."

As with the previous night, Meg delivered a list of places, on all sides of the town, for Harry to search.

Harry looked over the list with a heavy heart. "Will you watch over John for me? Tom will return with your food – ah, here he is. Thank you, Tom. I must look for Emilie Banter. She is our only hope for tomorrow."

As Harry rushed out of the rooms, Tom put the tray down and peered closely at Meg with a hard look on his mute face. She stared back at him defiantly.

"Well, idiot?"

As soon as Tom had put down the tray and gone, Meg went to the door and listened. When she was sure there was no one there she slipped out of the door and down the staircase.

IV

Maude banged a plate of food down on the floor in front of Emilie. Emilie looked at her.

"What is it Maude? Has something happened?"

"No – yes – oh, I don't know. I am just being silly. I can't expect to rush around dressed as a boy and then expect men to fall in love with me."

Emilie laughed.

"Yes – you make an attractive lad. I can imagine you have some trouble from certain gentlemen in this college. Is that what has upset you? Or is there a certain young man who is *not* noticing you?"

"It's not that, it's his noticing someone *else*."

"Aha! I see the problem. Your heart dreams of someone who's heart desires another."

"I don't imagine it's his heart that desires her, but a far baser part of his body. She's doing all those things that pretty women do and he's like a fish on a hook. It's disgusting..."

Emilie laughed at Maude's fury.

"I'm sorry, I know I shouldn't laugh. Is she pretty?"

"You know her – it is your friend Meg."

"Meg? Where is she?"

"She is hiding safely in another part of the college, but she's playing all those womanly games on my friend Harry – and I don't like it!"

Emilie raised her eyebrows. "Hmm. If it's Meg then I can understand your worry. She is a very attractive girl to the gentlemen and she is very good at the game too. That's why we work together. But he'll come round, don't you worry. When gentlemen have finished with women like us, they return to women like you."

Maude saw the cloud that drifted across Emilie's face.

"Do you ever wish to live a different life, Emilie?"

"There is no other life for women like me. Not unless someone chooses to rescue us from it."

Emilie smiled suddenly, a wide smile that lit up her face.

"But until they do, I will teach you!" she announced, "Come, sit down."

V

Meg returned to John's rooms with her brief absence undetected and bent over the bed. She shook John and slapped his face gently.

"John! Wake up! Come on, John, just a little."

John groaned and stirred. His eyes flickered on Meg and he tried to move, but could not. She produced a small green bottle from her pocket.

"A little drink, John. Come on now, just a sip or two..." Meg put her hand behind his head and lifted him slightly.

Hearing her command from somewhere deep inside a dark, echoing well, John obligingly drank a little of the sweet liquid. It slid easily over his tongue and before he passed out again he was aware of a slight metallic taste back of his throat.

VI

In Paradise Street, two large men banged at the door of the Irish witch, Mrs. O'Flaherty. When there was no response, they put their shoulder against it and broke in. Although they could see that they were too late – Mrs. O'Flaherty was gone – they searched the house anyway. They smashed pots of herbs and flowers on the floor, turned the table over and destroyed everything they could. When they were finished the two went back to the man who had sent them.

"No one there, lord. We were too late."

The Prelate thumped the wall with his fist, drawing blood that distracted him from the pain in his face.

"I'll find her. I'll find that witch and her devil children and hang them all!"

Chapter 8

I

THE DAY BEFORE CHRISTMAS dawned bright and clear. A cold wind had blown away all trace of the fog in the night and the city shone gloriously in the winter sun.

As he prepared himself for the trial, the Prelate was satisfied that all would be well. Although the girl had still not been found, he had placed guards around the college to make it impossible for her to enter. It was enough. They were safe.

At that same moment, elsewhere in the college, a soft voice woke Emilie from her comfortable sleep. She opened an eye to see Maude, dressed in an embroidered morning coat, her hair flowing down her back. Emilie sat up abruptly.

"Will you look at that? It would seem that you are ready to do battle, Lady Maude?"

"What do you think?"

She twirled around holding the sides of her coat.

"I think you are a beauty, Maude Mansfield. But I also think that coat is beautiful and I have half a mind to steal it from you and run."

"If John survives today, Emilie, I will make him buy such a coat for you."

"So that I can wear it to my execution?"

"I will do everything in my power to prevent that happening, Emilie."

II

If the Great Hall had seemed full for the announcement of the Duke's scholar five days before, it was nothing compared to today. The whole town was interested in the trial, and the guards on the college gates let through any who paid them well enough, all the while scrutinising their faces to check that Emilie was not among them.

The noisy crowd fell silent as the side door opened and the main players entered the Hall. The Duke was a different man to the one of five days before. It was the soldier, not the statesman who came in. His face was set in stone. As the Duke sat down, Edgar Hardridge hovered behind the Duke's chair, looking satisfied.

Dean Mansfield took his place at the centre of proceedings, his daughter Jane standing behind his right shoulder. The last few days had not been kind to Jane. She had slept little, worried a great deal and looked the worse for it. The red velvet was not a good choice – it did not help her complexion today. Edgar had been a frequent visitor to reassure her that the villain de Courcy would be brought to justice, once and for all, which had done nothing to make Jane's mood better.

Although she could not love a thief, Jane had loved John de Courcy. She wished she had Maude's faith in his innocence, but if she were truthful, she did not. She knew that John was a poor man. Edgar's whisperings had not helped: John had been seen coming out of Mrs. Munsby's house early in the morning! John had been seen talking to a prostitute! John had drunk so much that he had lost consciousness in Master Macebius's rooms! Edgar had made sure that Jane heard it all.

In short, Jane's heart was broken.

As the Prelate appeared in the Hall any remnant of noise from the crowd dissolved instantly into silence. He was someone who inspired more awe and fear than the Dean, more even than the Duke, especially among those in the crowd who kept their illegal religion hidden. He was dressed in ceremonial black robes, a black scarf covering the worst of his face. He took the seat of the prosecutor to the left of the dias.

"Call John de Courcy!" cried the University bailiff.

John, who had finally awoken only a couple of hours previously, appeared with Harry and Master Macebius. The Dean gestured to the two chairs where John and Macebius sat, while Harry stood behind, tall, proud and resolute. He looked for Maude, but his spirit plunged as he remembered their last encounter. What a fool he had been!

The Prelate got to his feet and cleared his throat. The harsh tones of his voice rang out across the Hall.

"We are come together to try the case of the nominated Duke's scholar, John de Courcy, discovered with his patron's ducal ring in his pocket."

He went through the facts of the case, his tone of voice allowing no doubt about John's guilt. He finished by saying "The evidence is simple and irrefutable. It is clear to us that John de Courcy must be stripped of his scholar's prize, and executed like the common thief he is."

The Prelate sat down again, his face alive with sneering satisfaction. The crowd whispered to each other like a field of wheat rustling in the wind. Macebius got to his feet and adjusted his robes. He cleared his throat. The crowd fell silent.

"These are terrible attacks upon the name of John de Courcy, a young man I have known for many years, a young man who has in all those years shown only honesty, diligence, intelligence, and virtue. My lord Prelate says the facts of the case are simple, but are they? What *evidence* do we have that the ring disappeared when the Duke fell off his horse?"

Macebius looked around at the Duke, his eyebrows dramatically raised.

"Well, your lordship?"

"I cannot remember the ring upon my finger when I rode in from the meadow."

"Nor I!" added Edgar.

Macebius raised his head and fixed Edgar with his eye.

"I would ask Sir Edgar Hardridge to remain silent, until asked to speak. Your time will come, Sir Edgar, believe me."

Edgar tried to look disdainfully at his philosophy master, but could not quite manage it. Macebius's tone had made the hairs on the back of his neck stand up.

"But then – I cannot remember the ring *not* being upon my finger either," added the Duke.

"Call Brane, the stable boy!" Macebius commanded.

Brane was brought in front of the crowd, looking uncomfortable in his clean clothes. Under Macebius' prompting, he described how he had helped the Duke down from his horse and how he had felt the ring dig into his shoulder.

"The boy's statement is true, Macebius," said the Duke. "I cannot vouch for the ring, and I would rather he had not revealed my difficulties getting off a horse to the entire population of Oxford, but it is true."

The crowd laughed at this, Macebius raising his hands to quiet them. Brane was dismissed and joined the front of the crowd, blushing.

III

Outside the college, the guards still kept to their posts, their vigilance more relaxed now that the trial had started. The only person to come to the college gates now was the coal merchant with his usual delivery of coal for the college fires.

"So!" Macebius continued, "As we know, the Duke then retired to his chambers in the company of two ladies to care for his injuries."

The crowd erupted in shouts and whistles, but the Duke jumped to his feet and stopped them with a resounding:

"Silence! If you cannot listen without such stupidity you will all be ejected from the Hall. This is a court of law, not a playhouse."

"You have already said," Macebius continued, "that the girls and the room were searched most completely, which is why you believe that the ring had been taken earlier. Did anyone else come or go from the chamber in that time?"

"Only the mute servant boy, who brought wine and cakes."

"You saw the boy?"

"Why don't we call the boy and ask him?" said the Prelate with a thin smile.

"Aye – call him," agreed the Duke.

Tom duly appeared through the door and stood at the edge of the court, looking terrified. The bailiff approached him with the Bible, but the Prelate stopped him.

"The boy cannot speak, Bailiff, so he cannot pronounce the oath. But he is a good boy and will tell the truth, won't you, Tom?"

Tom nodded, looking terrified. Macebius shifted on his seat but said nothing for the moment.

The Prelate fixed Tom with his uncovered eye.

"Now, Tom, no one's going to hurt you. We just need to ask you some questions. Do you remember the day, five days ago, when you were asked to take wine and cakes to the Duke's room?"

Tom nodded excitedly.

"When you stood at the door Tom, did you see the emerald ring upon the chest, as the Duke has said?"

Tom raised his eyebrows, shrugged and shook his head.

"Did one of the women in the room give *you* the ring, Tom?"

Tom shook his head vigorously again.

"And did you see anything else, Tom, that might be of interest?"

Tom shook his head. The Prelate smiled a tight, cruel smile at him. "Why then you may retire, Tom."

"You may not retire, Tom!" shouted Macebius. Tom jumped out of his skin but stayed where he was. "I also have questions for you."

Macebius took a Bible from his bag and walked slowly towards Tom, who stared at the book as if it were a knife. Macebius stopped and looked at the Prelate.

"A cheap trick, my lord Prelate. And one that does you no favours. Tom may not be able to *speak* the oath, but he can lay his hand upon the book and agree to speak the truth, so help him God, can you not, Tom?"

Tom cowered and nodded at Macebius.

"While answering my questions, Tom, I would like you to keep your hand on this Holy Bible. This is *not* the Bible of King Henry, Tom, this is a Bible dating from 1525. Do you know what that means, Tom?"

Tom stared at Macebius, terrified.

"It means, Tom, that it is a Bible of the Church of Rome. As a member of that church, Tom, if you lie while your hand is upon this book, you will be damned for eternity. There will be no absolution for you, do you understand?"

Tom nodded vigorously.

"My Lord of Gloucester, I protest!" shouted the Prelate. "What grounds does Macebius have for these accusations against this poor boy?"

Macebius eyed the Prelate.

"I suggest sir, that you do not tempt me..."

The Duke waved his hand dismissively at the Prelate and turned to listen to Macebius once more.

"Now Tom, I'd like you to take a moment to look at John de Courcy sitting there."

Tom lifted his head and looked at John, who nodded kindly and smiled at the terrified lad.

"Now, Tom, with your hand upon the Holy Bible and God's truth in your heart: did you see the Duke's ring that day?"

Tom nodded his head mournfully. A murmur went through the crowd. The Prelate's flashed furiously at him, but Tom looked steadily at the Bible.

"Did one of the women in the Duke's chamber hand you the ring, Tom?"

Tom nodded again. No one breathed.

"Would you recognise her, Tom?"

Tom nodded.

"And who did you give the ring to?"

Tom's hand was visibly shaking on the Bible. He stared at the floor, tears dropping from the end of his bent nose. Edgar jumped to his feet.

"Leave the poor boy alone! This is not fair, Macebius. He is only a mute fool."

Tom lifted his head, his lips pursed determinedly, then lifted his other hand and pointed at Sir Edgar, whose eyes opened as large as saucers. The crowd could not control themselves, they burst out in comment upon this new turn of events.

"Silence!" Macebius ordered, "Why did you do this terrible thing, Tom? You are a good man, I know it. Why did you help steal the ring?"

Tom pointed at Sir Edgar and mimicked a person cutting his throat. Then he pointed at the Prelate and then at the Bible, his face so frightened that the crowd grew silent again.

"Are you saying that Sir Edgar beat you and threatened your life, and that the Lord Prelate promised you eternal damnation if you did not do as they said?"

Tom nodded, tears flooding down his face.

IV

"So now, the women. Do we have the two women?"

"We have one sir, Meg Marber."

Meg appeared, took the oath and looked over

the crowd, her chest filling with excitement at being in front of so many people. She winked at Edgar, but the wink was noticed by the Duke whose brow furrowed.

"You have heard the evidence of the boy Tom, Meg Marber. Is it true?"

"No. It most certainly is not. That boy is a liar. He is a friend of that de Courcy."

John looked shocked at her change in sympathies. Harry was less surprised by her change of heart.

"The boy came to the door, as he says, but beyond that he is lying. I can assure you no ring went out of the room."

"Were you the one who answered the door?"

Meg looked uncomfortable for a moment.

"No, that was my friend Emilie."

"And we still have no sign of this Emilie?"

"No, sir." Harry admitted sorrowfully, "No sign."

"Yes, sir! A sign!" Maude appeared from the crowd and climbed on to the platform.

Unlike the last time Harry had seen her, she was dressed in her finest, deep purple dress. Her hair cascaded down her back, and she looked in every way a lady.

"What sign, Mistress Maude?" asked Macebius.

"If you will promise to treat her with leniency for her testimony, sir, I will show you to the other girl – Emilie Banter. I could not bring her myself as the danger was too great. Will *you* come with me to accompany her to the court?"

The Prelate had turned a strange shade of grey, fitting with his clothes. He half rose.

"Not you, sir!" shouted Maude. "I will not have you near my rooms."

The crowd could contain themselves no more and erupted with excitement, while Maude and Macebius, accompanied by a small guard of bailiffs and stewards went to collect Emilie from her hiding place.

As she entered the Great Hall, the whole assembly were on their feet with excitement. Jane's eyes opened wide and she called crossly to her sister, "Maude! She is in my dress!"

Edgar looked a little shocked as Emilie appeared in person, looking demure and beautiful, but smiled his most charming smile at her. She did not smile back at him.

Macebius called for silence.

"So, Emilie Banter. A whole town searching for you and yet you escape? Well done, Mistress. You are obviously a resourceful young woman."

"Not I, sir, or only part of it. It was Maude Mansfield here who saved me from the gentlemen who planned to poison me."

At this the crowd erupted with cries of "Shame!" and "Murderers!"

Macebius boomed over the crowd,

"Quiet! If there is one more disturbance, I will have you all removed from the Hall. We will establish who the other players in this plot are presently, but for now, we are here to establish only whether John de Courcy is guilty of stealing the Duke of Gloucester's ring. Is it correct that you, Mistress Banter, were in the Duke's rooms on the afternoon of the 20th day of December?"

"I was, sir. With Meg Marber, sir."

"And can you enlighten this court at all as to the case of the missing ring, Mistress Banter?"

"I can, sir. I took it, sir."

It was difficult, but the whole crowd knew it was essential to stay utterly silent to hear the rest of the story.

"You?"

"Yes, sir, I took it on the orders of Sir Edgar Hardridge, and when Tom knocked upon the door, as was arranged, I passed the ring to him. Then he handed it to Sir Edgar, who had a plan to secrete it on John de Courcy's person and destroy his reputation."

"And can I ask," Macebius paused, "why you would agree to do this for Sir Edgar? Are you in the habit of stealing?"

"No, sir, I may not be the most virtuous of maids, but he said that if I stole the ring and kept quiet about it, I would be Lady Hardridge. So I did. But now I've not kept quiet about it."

"May I venture to ask why?"

"Because when I was imprisoned above the Lord Prelate's rooms, sir, I heard them say they were going to kill me."

"This is outrageous!" The Prelate had jumped to his feet and shouted at the Court. "This whore is part of a plot! She lies! They always lie, these whores."

Emilie was quite used to abuse and was unmoved by it. She drew back the arm of her gown to expose the injuries on her wrist.

"I would not invent these, sir. These wounds are real and inflicted upon me by your men, as you well know."

"Lies! All lies!"

"Sir Edgar," Macebius continued, "if you would like to come forward and take the oath?"

Macebius produced the Catholic Bible he had used for Tom.

"Would you like to swear in your own faith, Edgar? It might encourage you to speak the truth?"

Edgar's nostrils flared and his eyes narrowed at his benign old philosophy master.

"Now, Sir Edgar Hardridge. What have you to say to all this?"

Edgar could be seen to be gulping in mouthfuls of air.

"Lies," he managed, "all the lies of my enemies and whores. I am the Duke of Gloucester's nephew.

Why on earth would I want to steal from him and put the blame of that theft upon another?"

"You were the next in line to be the Duke's scholar, were you not?"

"I was, but that is not enough of a reason to destroy another man. I am a gentleman. I would not dream of doing the things I have been accused of here today by these whores and fools."

"Yet why would they choose to lie? A girl would not say that she stole from a Duke unless that were true. Emilie Banter is facing execution for what she has said today."

"Uncle!" Edgar was on his feet again. "You cannot believe these whores and villains over me. Will you silence them now, and send de Courcy to gaol where he should rightfully be?"

The Duke looked sideways at Edgar and slowly got to his feet.

"As far as I can see, there are whores on both sides, Edgar, and you in the middle of them, as always. Call the dark-haired one again – what's her name? Meg?"

Meg reappeared on the dias.

"You are still on oath, young woman, although I presume that means little to you?"

"I am a God-fearing, devout girl, sir."

"And I am the Queen of Sheba," answered the Duke. "Tell me, my girl, has Edgar promised you marriage as well?"

The crowd laughed aloud at this and Meg glared indignantly at their jeering.

"He has! And he loves me! Not Emilie. She always thinks she is better than me, but Edgar loves *me*, not her. I am to be married to Sir Edgar Hardridge, he has promised me so!"

"Edgar?"

"Nonsense, uncle. They are all mad."

Meg looked stricken.

"Edgar!"

Edgar looked completely unperturbed.

"Enough of this charade!" shouted the Duke. "I can well believe you promised these young women marriage, Edgar, although without witnesses they cannot hold you to your word, as you well know. What I find harder to believe, but am beginning to see, is that you would steal from your own uncle in order to be rid of your rival in life and love –

for we mustn't forget the presence of Mistress Jane Mansfield in all this. Has he promised you marriage too, Jane?"

Jane flushed furiously and stared at the ground, shaking her head, although it was true, Edgar had talked of marriage with her and, although she had certainly not returned his affection, she had listened.

"It does not appear to me that John de Courcy is the guilty party here," the Duke continued. "But we have many questions to ask of the lord Prelate and my nephew."

"My lord!" the Prelate was on his feet, his mouth snarling in fury. "This is all nonsense. Show me the evidence of drugging and poisoning."

Macebius came forward with a goblet which he held towards the Duke.

"This is the goblet of wine that Sir Edgar poured for John de Courcy yesterday morning. John did not rise again until a little while ago. If you care to taste a drop of the residue, you may recognise the taste of Gravidor, a potion made from a particular mix of herbs and flowers to make people sleep."

The Duke sniffed the goblet and gingerly put his finger in the remainder,

"But what proof is this?" shouted the Prelate. "Anyone could have drugged the boy."

"And Emilie? But he is correct," the Duke said. "What proof is there?"

"I am proof, sir!" A figure stepped forward out of the crowd. Every exposed bit of her face and hair was black with coal dust. "My name is Susan O'Flaherty, sir. The Gravidor was bought from me. Men were sent to harm me and my children, sir, but we escaped. I was forced to hide, and entered the college in a coal sack, so I excuse my appearance."

The Duke's eyes shone with merriment at the sight of her.

"I had never expected such entertainment from this trial! You are the maker of potions then?"

"I am, sir. Two persons have bought the Gravidor in the last month, sir, only two. One is standing there..." she pointed at Croke, whose face drained of the little colour it had, "and the other is the wench called Meg Marber. And he–" she pointed again at Croke, "also stole arsenic from my jar when he thought I was not looking."

The Duke threw up his hands.

"Enough! The circle draws to a close. One fact is clear: John de Courcy is guilty of no crime. Guards, take the Lord Prelate to his rooms, with Croke and Sir Edgar Hardridge. They shall stay under guard until I have put this case to the Queen. Put the women, Emilie Banter and Meg Marber, and the boy Tom, under guard also. I shall deal with them soon. John – you are indeed the Duke of Gloucester's Scholar. Go in complete freedom! Your honour is restored. Maude Mansfield, I must keep a word for you. I am no fool. I see that this case was saved not by the lawyers and the intellectuals, but by you. If it were possible to have a woman as my scholar it would be you, Miss Mansfield, for you are a rare type of woman."

"I follow the example of my sovereign Elizabeth, my lord."

"And she shall hear of you, Miss Mansfield. She shall hear of you."

Epilogue

JOHN AND HARRY walked by the side of the frozen river, in the Meadows to the north of the city. At this time of year the Meadow was abandoned, the two friends the only figures on the horizon.

"The Duke is right, I am a fraud, Harry, and undeserving of the Scholar's prize, if common sense and intelligence are the measure of the place," said John.

Harry laughed.

"It is true, Johnny, that without Maude it is most likely we would have been lost. And to think I said such hurtful things to her, half-believing that two-faced whore Meg Marber."

"But Maude cannot be given the Duke's scholarship, however much she is the true solver of this riddle, so it must stay with me, and I am happy for it."

"And happy with her sister?"

"I will think on that subject, Harry. Jane was not always kind, and did not have the belief in me that Maude had. Yet they both had the same evidence before them. Maybe I should ask Maude to be my wife?"

"What!" Harry exploded, turning furiously on his friend.

John burst out laughing and clapped his arm around his friend's shoulder.

"Ha! I see you too have a point of weakness in the Mansfield family? Do not worry – I will leave young Maude for you. For me, I am in no hurry to marry. If Jane Mansfield shows herself to have a little more faith in me than it previously appeared, then I might look at her again."

"Listen to you! You might 'look at her again' indeed? I do believe I should have left you to your fate and let you rot in gaol..."

And so the friends walked on by the side of the River Thames as the sun began to set on Christmas Eve.

If you enjoyed this book, don't miss the
other titles from the **paper planes** collection.

Here is an excerpt from:

Distant Echo

Janice Hally

Chapter 1

COGITO ERGO SUM. *Je pense, donc je suis. I think, therefore I am.*

Lost in my thoughts, I looked out of the train window and saw the curve of the viaduct ahead and a spectacular gorge below. I suddenly realised that the train was speeding through the heart of the South West toward Toulouse, and I would soon be face-to-face with the enigma of Marilyn Jensen.

I think, therefore I am.

Establishing that we exist is a start, but Descartes didn't continue the discourse with the question: "I am... but *who* am I?"

When I was a student, this was always the

source of much debate. Psychology, psychiatry, medicine, philosophy, religion: all proffered theories, but none could completely explain the essence of a person's individuality, their personality, their *spirit*.

What made me so different from Philippe Rohart, for example? We had taken the same classes, passed the same examinations, gained the same qualifications. So what had motivated him to create his empire within the medical system, but compelled me to escape it? And why, since he had little but contempt for my choices, had he telephoned me first thing this morning, anxious for my help?

The little buffet cart rattled to a stop beside me and I bought a coffee. As the water dripped through the filter into the plastic cup, I thought back to eight o'clock that morning in my apartment in Paris. Philippe had used his secretary to place the call. He did it to ensure that I realised how important he was these days. She had informed me that "Dr Philippe Rohart, the *Chef de Clinique* of Hopital Casselardit in Toulouse" was on the line, and paused as if giving me time to stand to attention before announcing that she would connect me to him.

I almost expected a musical fanfare, but after a brief pause Philippe came on the line, breathless, hesitant "Hello? Alexandre? Hello?"

I detected a small tremor as he observed the pleasantries of asking how I was, and what I was doing these days. He was doing his best to be sociable, but it was clear that he had a favour to ask and was nervous about introducing the subject. I enjoyed prolonging his agony by telling him about my latest book. Even across the phone line I could hear that he was congratulating me on my success through clenched teeth.

Finally, I allowed him to divulge his business. He launched into the story of Marilyn Jensen, an American tourist who had fallen from a mountain path at Saint-Cirq Lapopie.

"She was in a coma after the fall," he told me, "now she has regained consciousness, but is exhibiting retrograde amnesia."

"So she can't recollect the accident. That's not unusual."

"More than that, Alexandre. It's global. It's not

just the accident that's a blank. She can't remember anything about herself. Doesn't recognise her fiancé. He was at her side while she was comatose, but since she regained consciousness, we're not permitting him to enter her room because it's too perturbing for her. She has no idea who he is. I'd like you to come and have a look at her."

I've encountered amnesia often in patients. It can take many forms. It can be caused by trauma, physical or mental. It can be caused by tumours, cerebral seizures, or degenerative disease.

Sometimes the memories are still there, hidden in some cranial cache, and they can be accessed again as if recovering data from a faulty computer's hard drive. Sometimes the memories, and the person that they formed, are lost forever.

I had studied in the USA, and I assumed Philippe was calling me in because he wanted someone proficient in English to help with the case of this young American woman. But then he explained how it was more complicated than I realised.

"There was a slight cut on the left side of her head. No fractures showed in X-rays. We're doing a CT scan to see if there is any injury to the left hemisphere of her brain. At the moment, she seems to have a form of aphasia. She cannot comprehend or speak her native English."

I didn't understand: if she had lost the ability to talk, how was she communicating with them about her amnesia?

"It's the strangest thing, Alexandre," Philippe continued, "she understands and can speak perfectly... *in French*."

ABOUT THE AUTHOR

PHILIPPA BOSTON is a writer and journalist who lives in Oxford. As a journalist, she is a columnist and arts writer for the *Oxford Times*. She has published a history of St. Clare's College in Oxford and has extensively studied the city's medieval period. Her short stories have been performed on Radio Oxford, and at the Pegasus Theatre, as well as being published in *The Lady*. She is a member of Oxford Voices writing group.

The Fortunes of John de Courcy
on www.paperplanes.fr:

- the audio version read by Hester Wilcox
- Philippa Boston talks about writing *The Fortunes of John de Courcy*
- more about English society in the 16th century